Kayla:
A Modern-Day Princess

Deedee Cummings

Copyright © 2021 Deedee Cummings

All rights reserved. No part of this book may be reproduced, stored, or transmitted by any means—whether auditory, graphic, mechanical, or electronic—without written permission of both publisher and author, except in the case of brief excerpts used in critical articles and reviews. Unauthorized reproduction of any part of this work is illegal and is punishable by law.

ISBN: 978-1-951218-06-5 (sc)
ISBN: 978-1-951218-07-2 (e)

Because of the dynamic nature of the Internet, any web addresses or links contained in this book may have changed since publication and may no longer be valid. The views expressed in this work are solely those of the author and do not necessarily reflect the views of the publisher, and the publisher hereby disclaims any responsibility for them.

Interior Image Credit: Charlene Mosley

makeawaymedia.com
deedeecummings.com

@makeawaymedia
@authordeedeecummings

Other books by the author

Love Is...
Think of it Like This!
My Trip to the Beach
My Dad's Job
Heart
I Want to Be a Bennett Belle
If A Caterpillar Can Fly, Why Can't I?
Like Rainwater
In The Nick of Time
This Is The Earth

Kayla is a gift.

She is just like you.

She is happy, and she has hopes and dreams.

Every day her mom wakes her up and says, "What's your plan today? Every day you have to have a plan. A plan gives you hope, and hope gives you dreams.
So, what's your plan today?"

Most of the time, Kayla only sees her mom in the mornings.

Her mom works very late, and by the time she gets home, it is usually way past Kayla's bedtime. Tonight, however, she is waiting up for her mom because daddy said it was okay.

Her mom had called home earlier in the day and said that she had big news to share. Even though it was nowhere near her birthday, Kayla hoped it had something to do with getting a present.

Just as she was dreaming of all the toys she wanted, Kayla heard the garage door open. She ran to the window and screamed,

"Hello Mr. Moon! Mama is home!"

Kayla wanted to race downstairs. She could not help but kick her feet up and down in excitement. She walked to her doorway and pressed her ear close to the door.

She could hear her mom climbing the stairs. Like a lightning bolt, she went from the door back to her bed in a second!

Kayla's mom beamed with pride as she opened the door.

Her mom gave her a big hug and said, "How is my sweet little princess in her tower?"

Kayla said, "I am good mama. Do you have a present for me?"

"No, I did not say I had a present. I said I have big news."

"What's the big news?" Kayla wondered out loud.

"I got a promotion."

"Mom, that's wonderful! It's what you worked so hard for."

"Yes, I have. We all have, really. And, I got a present for you."

"Yes, yes, yes! I knew it."

Kayla clapped her hands in excitement.

From her work bag, Kayla's mom pulled out a sparkly tiara fit for a princess.

"What is this for, mom?"

"This is for you. I want you to wear it proudly. Always believe, and know how special you are. People will be mean sometimes, and they will try to tell you differently. Don't you pay them any mind! Do you hear me? I want you to always be treated special, like royalty, because that is what you are."

She then placed the little crown on top of Kayla's head.

It fit perfectly.

"Now, I have a secret to share with you, little one." Kayla's eyes opened wide with anticipation.

"The best promotion I ever received was the day I became your mom." Mom and daughter looked at each other. In Kayla's eyes, her mom saw all of the hopes and dreams she ever had. A journey that, in this moment, made all the hard work worth it. In her mom's eyes, Kayla saw her hopes and dreams for her future. A role model to follow.

No matter how big or scary her dreams may be...

...Kayla would find a way.

She would **make** a way.

Kayla went to sleep with her little tiara on her head and her favorite doll in her arms.

She dreamed of her future, her wishes, and her hopes.

She thought, "This world is a beautiful and magical place."

That night, Kayla dreamed of what her life could be. She promised herself she would see as much of the world as she possibly could.

She knew she had to have a plan.
The world would be her stage.

She was happy as she slept because she was hopeful.

Meet the Team

This is an #OwnVoices project. This series was written by a Black author and is being illustrated by a Black artist. This is a rare combination.

Even now, we are still battling gatekeepers in the publishing industry who decide what stories are worthy of being told and who will illustrate them. Characters of color are not the only area severely underrepresented; authors and illustrators of color are too.

#OwnVoices is a movement that began on Twitter, but it has now extended far beyond that platform. People of all backgrounds have a right to tell their own stories. Marginalized populations have historically been shut out when it comes to creating art that reflects their own experiences. Even when someone else tells your story well, it is not the same as you personally having the freedom and the ability to teach the world about your own journey.

The most authentic story is told by the one who lived it.

Deedee Cummings - Author

As a therapist, attorney, author, and CEO of Make A Way Media, Deedee Cummings has spent more than two decades working within the family support field. Much of her writing is reflective of her experience working with kids in therapeutic foster care. All sixteen of Deedee's diverse picture books, poetry books, and workbooks are not only fun for kids and adults to read, they also work to teach coping skills, reinforce the universal message of love, encourage mindfulness, and facilitate inclusion for all. Deedee is an award-winning author whose work has appeared in national publications such as Essence Magazine, USA Today, Forbes, and the Huffington Post. Deedee resides in Louisville, Kentucky.

Charlene Mosley - Illustrator

Born in Berlin, Charlene Mosley is a fine artist, illustrator, and muralist, who works in oil and watercolor. Charlene has exhibited in both national and international exhibitions. In 2016, Charlene was one of the contributing artists of *Loving Vincent*, the first fully-painted, Oscar-nominated feature film. Mosley's current work discusses the 21st- century media-driven society and its relationship to technology and nature. She resides in San Diego.

The Mission of Make A Way Media

Make A Way Media was founded by Deedee Cummings in 2014 and focuses on creating positive and diverse media images and publications. This company is the driving force behind the Kayla series. To date, Make A Way Media has successfully supported the creation and publication of eleven diverse books for children.

We are committed to ensuring that all children have access to diverse books because we know that reading develops esteem, efficacy, and empathy in children. Make A Way Media has gifted over 1,000 books to homes, families, community centers, churches, and schools that are severely lacking in diverse children's books. In addition to donating hundreds of books each year, Make A Way Media is also an active supporter of the It Pays to Read program, donating more than 10% of all proceeds to this literacy awareness nonprofit.

It Pays to Read is a program that works with at-risk youth to improve literacy skills because we believe literacy is a fundamental human right. Literacy affects every area of our lives from our ability to apply for a job, read a prescription bottle, or clearly articulate our wants and needs. Reading changes lives. It Pays to Read accomplishes these goals through working with kids on improving their behavioral health and soft job skills, while literally paying kids to read. Make A Way Media and It Pays to Read have similar missions in also recognizing that children are far more likely to become engaged in a book, and will continue to read more, when the books have characters who look like them or reflect their experiences.

In the children's publishing industry, books are eight times more likely to feature an animal as the protagonist than a person of color. Make A Way Media is not only working to address this divide by creating books that portray diverse characters throughout the story, but also highlighting these characters as leaders. Kayla: A Modern-Day Princess shows Black and Brown girls that they can be leaders too and that princesses come in all colors.

It is important to note that books with black and brown characters are not made solely for black and brown children. All children need to read books and see other positive media and imagery as it lessens the divide between cultures, increases our understanding and empathy towards one another, and combats an overdose of steady negative stereotypes and imagery in our daily media exposure.